Things We Might Miss

New and Collected Poems

Susan Stevens

Finishing Line Press
Georgetown, Kentucky

Things We Might Miss

New and Collected Poems

Publisher: Leah Maines

Editor: Christen Kincaid

Cover Art: Aerial photo of Sunset Crater volcano near Flagstaff, Arizona by Eric
Gofreed with pilot Ted Grussing. Reprinted with permission of Eric Gofreed.

Author Photo: Mario Acevedo

Cover Design: Elizabeth Maines McCleavy

Printed in the USA on acid-free paper.
Order online: www.finishinglinepress.com
                      also available on amazon.com

Author inquiries and mail orders:
Finishing Line Press
P. O. Box 1626
Georgetown, Kentucky 40324
U. S. A.

Contents

For a writer I have met whose tolerance for ambiguity allows him special conversance—spontaneity, sympathy, awe—in a profusion of subjects

I

Forgive me if you read this, said James
Merrill in "Days of 1964," and I too—
peccavi—sometimes need to say it.

Subliminal: No Waiting Ever

Love without conversation is impossible.
Mortimer Adler

When I think of you
there's so much to think about
(biographical
extravaganza)—
it's that ratiocination
which
is
(it may be argued)
more lively
than actually touching
someone. Even more intimate.

I write poems at stoplights
and no, I don't want
to meet you across
a crowded room.
You are my idea
of the ideal person
to think about....
Stravinsky said,
"The more constraints
one imposes, the more
one frees oneself."
I can't tell all
of what you do to me
some of it is ineffable
some is untranslatable
and some is wayward.
You say reminiscing
is *masochism.* Nabokov
said that "the more you love
a memory, the stronger
and stranger it is."
I can't choose here
but will think about it

You, Somewhere

Feeling the distance
between us heady, keeping you
dreamily spiritual—I find
our dialogue visionary,
simply preposterous,
turning my senses
over and over in mad *eros.*

What finally happens
to the life of the mind?
Surely it is like you: somewhere.
Here I go, tripping again
in this faraway chaste discourse,
wrangling with disbelief
so palpable that I think
the you of us
is someone else.
And *somewhere,*
you with your usual ease
in learning the ropes
are again a quick study, seeing it
this way for perhaps the first time,
feeling the distance.

Ne Plus Ultra

Presence is more than just being there. —Malcolm Forbes

Being solitary is being alone well. —Alice Koller

Be where you are; otherwise you will miss your life. ·—the Buddha

Where I want you
is not close
is on a page
is not on a walk or a plane in a ship or even an Alfa Romeo
is in a dream or a film or the mail
but not on a hike or skates
in a court, café
or in a *tête-à-tête.*

Stay where you are—
I can always pull you off a shelf
or tune in an interview
as I praise the paradox:
hell-and-gone intimacy
shocked, finding its own level.

Men In Bars

were *not* the ones
I wanted to meet
in my twenties, or ever.
O, but in the library
was my idea
of a good man.
There, I could scan
the stacks for the bright guy
in 811.08 or 811 L95Yh
(and always with glasses—
they stirred me
as half-dressed
women did men),
position myself
around the corner
from his fixed reverie,
push a book
through to his side
and onto the floor—
then run around to
retrieve it and apologize.
I waited. I had to find out
if he was as intelligent
as he was meant to be.

Mindfulness

*You're like a plaintive melody
that never lets me be....*
                    Arthur Freed

Even angry, you would
see to your words with care.
You are impressive, you are erotic,
you are wildly undomesticated,
the most rational-emotive
man alive. You don't scare me.
The audience is ever more aroused
to attention: You might as well be back
in the classroom with that abiding vigor!
We see in the essays a mighty show
of candor, then for crying out loud,
it's your paradoxical shyness,
coming back like Lassie or Shane.
You make me think over my head
and let me wonder
not how you learned the language
so fast, but how soon you came to be
this lovingly articulate.

And That's Final

Undressing before
his face
on the cover
of his book
I trust
his eyes' unblinking
appraisal
his good taste to stay put
my letting well enough
alone
and the probity of distance.
No more heroes, I say

Immersion

Your words simmer
all around me,
a deep pool of astonishment—
then a complex network
of conceptual channels, then waves
one jump ahead of me.
I cannot swim.
The spindrift resembles the way
your presence might feel.
Once revived, I want to ask (no levity now):
Are you of our ongoing script really he, the writer,
not his secretary, assistant, colleague,
friend, relative, man on the street—
someone else? You will see now just how serious
is someone's inability to manage awe.

Moving from book to book,
I see we can manage parlance
apropos of mystery and fast currents,
even without the swimming bit.

I like our distance
and will get a yacht to expand it,
to sail through the secret,
sparking evanescence.

Building It Up

...*oxytocin is stimulated by everything from
holding hands, to feeling supported, to orgasm.*
Loretta Graziano Breuning

I want you to think of yourself as the man
nowhere to be found, and who rolled
the Sisyphean stone of desire uphill
for me where, curiously, it stayed put.
I want you to think of yourself
as the resuscitator of this brain's
circuit of pleasure-seekers
that hunt down willing receptors.
(Make that *eager* receptors.) I want you
to keep thinking, talking, writing,
wandering where you may,
always a friend to the proprieties and trust.
It's tantalizing when you stand
on ceremony.

Before It Gets There: The End of Postmortem Blues

If you don't know how to die, don't worry; Nature will tell you
what to do . . . don't bother your head about it.
Michel de Montaigne

His deathlike experience
might inform our own
approach. Please, let's have more
of the Stoic's *amor fati*
and *ars memoriae.* —It's just like passing out,
Montaigne tells us, which we anyhow
have been known to do with our heads
in his copious *Essays.*

Take a better attitude
to death, he advises;
it only happens once—
how bad can that be?
"If you have lived a day,
you have seen everything,"
Montaigne consoles.
Would you parry his words
assuring that our regrets
for loss and wishes and this life
lose all meaning (you'll be gone)
and cease to be mourned?

About Desire

Preferences are harmless; we can have as many as we want. . .[but] We have to see that everything we demand (and even get) eventually disappoints us.
          Charlotte Joko Beck, *Nothing Special*

If we have distance
our desire
won't let us demand,
much less get.
The delight lies in missing
something. Or someone. Yeats
said (was he thinking of love?),
"Be secret and exult,
because of all things known,
that is the most difficult."
In the garden we may spy something
we missed before—a thing we *must* have.
But the core of it's this: Demand satisfaction
in practice, exercise, action, and you attach
to dismay. Satisfaction is that glorious unspeakable
thing that freely comes to me arising from distance and missing
(in Kōshō Uchiyama's words, "when I open the hand of thought").

II

Sestina *Pro Tempore*

Finishing one installment of learning that—well,
blazed brightly, I totter and my mind
shuts down. The touchy choke of my thought
resists adjustment. Even fireworks in their many
fashions sputter. . . Volcanoes in
their glossy issue will burn out,

disgorge to repose. Ought I not to be played out?
Even a meteor blooms to terminus. You know, this well
may describe the ultimate state students everywhere are in.
For all the seduction of learning, my mind
is a flat, dry Kansas. This brings many
meditations on the intellect to mind: Remember when thinking

was fashionable? Being deep in thought
was in vogue, and competitive folks were out
there on television, hawking their wits on many
shows like *Jeopardy* and the *GE College Bowl.* It's well
to remember that education excited people, like passion. One's mind
was a status symbol then, in the '50s. The brainy sparring in

schools kept students where they should be: deep in
issues, well-read. All this modulated into the anti-thought
wave of the '60s, where the idea was to blank out your mind.
My god, minds were demolished in those days. And now, even literacy is out,
in favor of mechanical marvels. Now, dialogue seems unwell;
the apoplectic shifts of televised scenes assure that many

habitués will never again try reading for pleasure. Many.
In
well-
thought-
out
poems someone writes for Carnegie-Mellon or Lamont, the mind

risks itself upon the flat page (a dangerously good mind),
plush for someone's slow, embracing eyes (not that many,
but as long as there are some!). A poet misses out
without seductive thought; and what's missing now in
students is a passion. For banter. In thinking.
Can you say why even excitement won't excite them? Ah, well.

"Too many poets," said Frost, "delude themselves by thinking
the mind is dangerous and must be left out.
Well, the mind is dangerous and must be left in."

For the Concrete Man

The man with the black lunchbox
is thinking. He is all geometry
as he nears the site where he knows
he is on new ground.

This man, who eschewed
touch-typing, will stop at nothing
to use both hands as he lays concrete
in shuttering. A laborer now, he imagines
writing a book on the esthetics
of Quikrete
and the satisfaction of arduous toil,
when his hands might caress
the burl in a railroad tie
or a piece of honey onyx he found
by happenstance. He is heavy on irony,
and so is the prospect
of his contemplating aggregate, control joints,
braced 2x6 wood forms, concrete floating,
then gradually moving into passive solar
though he doesn't know it yet.

Next will be Xeriscape design,
placing gargantuan boulders,
creating abstract snakes out of concrete,
and designing a water wall.
He will be a sculptor and more.
This man will stop at nothing
to use the full range of his hands;
he has stopped at nothing
at every juncture,
at every turn of phrase.

Study in Yellow: Above Hell Canyon

Juniper steams its scent into Arizona's midday,
sunflowers swarming above the pungency to glimpse
a girl in mechanized flight. She imagines
the juniper as toxic; sunflowers lean
like rubbernecks at a disaster toward her
in sensational frenzy. She wants
to elude the juniper

Sunflowers have garish eyes on long stems
lurching. *The only girl on this road* slams
shut vents pouring acrid air, with nowhere
left to catch an innocent breath. Inhaling
by degrees, she begins to realize
she is driving down this road away
from him, into a cunning nature

Mantle

Alaska, March 1964

The family savors their refuge on an Oregon shore;
wavelets curl the sand in easy scallops
then ebb, shyly. This company's on sure ground—propped
on bedrolls, severed at last from the automated stream
of funereal parades, transports, tourist cavalcades.

The only disturbance here is two thousand miles away,
on midwestern farms where birds and livestock revolt
in their own solitude, a riot as yet unmarked by men—
and too late for the clan on Beverly Beach:
Would they have believed the water's growing corruption?

The inoffensive waves, more sinned against than sinning, feel
a troubled shudder, whiplash from jarred vertical planes
as permafrost layers jolt in that time of year up north
called (ironically, now) "break-up." There, unstable clay
will let slip homes into that part of Cook Inlet
known as Turnagain; a theater marquee will sink
thirty feet to street level; and a prominent lawyer
will run naked from a bath house to join a human chain,
deft drunks in the street.

Good Friday darkens doorsteps, prophets' eyes.
Children watch telephone poles careening, and know
they've never moved before. Other things move that shouldn't:
There's the Easter ham that's stealing
out the sprung oven door; train tracks becoming unfeasible
zigzags; the careless shatter and mix of liquor
as barkeeps clutch at premium brands; the landslide
of books, shoes, food, everywhere inside,
mimicking the shift of earth's shelves.

This land, where everything arrives six months late,
is the first to have an 8.5-Richter-scaled heaving
for five minutes during Happy Hour, when 2-for-1

means more to some than running—running from or into a thing
like never before: the end of *terra firma,* where nothing
you know will empower you; where a tape-recorded
conference in a government high-rise will get instead (before
electricity fails for two days) the cavernous sounds
the word *groan* has always suggested, but no one's heard
before this day. Families all over town are holding onto walls
and each other, thinking this is it, a la *Revelations,*
because they can even see the mountains moving,
and *know* they've never moved before.

Side by side, the family sleeps on a beach, safe
from terrorists, but not the aberrations of nature.
Who wouldn't think that the last whim of all that troop,
before drowsing, was to drift out to sea?

Spanning

Over grits and apple-buttered toast
that year we read aloud, in
turn, from books we'd cached
in winter—*At Play in the Fields*
of the Lord and *River Notes*—
while light refracted through
old lace and beveled glass
of the 1918 duplex
to fall on your circa 1965-origin
face that pulled joy
(like nurtured babes)
from the page which held you
absolutely taut and childlike
in a year and time
you seemed to thrive,
having franchise in our own house
to do all as you saw fit,
and managing the fittest coupling
I'd known in my scarce
own 43 years

Hazard

If you have been
there before it's still
the first time like
accretions surrounding
a burl new layers
incipient each time
new eyes plumb
yours in genesis
of where you have
already been
can't guess or
guarantee the
outcome is new no
matter how ancient
the humanity there are
no comparisons to be
made no connections
that will help
in virgin soil all
is primitive riotous
your meeting someone
else is primeval
and you must not
presuppose for that
is barbarism or drift
all is intentional
your eyes will say
all anyone presently
needs to know

Its Own Magic

For me, you are nothing but the you that is within
my world, within the universal self as my world.
Kōshō Uchiyama

When I call you
in my head
I use your first name
very lightly
since it is shocking to do so
even to me
(I know you
I don't know you)—
and important
that you not hear
this presumption
bumping into your ordinary
but whole, complete privacy.

Once in a hotel at 4 a. m.
you wrote *You are asleep*
and I found this intimate
that you should say it
but still your first name
only has conversance
in my head
I know you don't know you
there's a *koan* in there
I must face
without thinking about it

Maple Leaves and Moon

From where you are you cannot
see these swirling maple leaves

in their redundant heaps about my feet
(perhaps the gambel oak litters

your lawn in like profusion); but moving
my eyes just, say, three yards on a horizontal

from the maple's crown, there is that white
hemisphere, *bas relief* on blue, which

you *can* see. From where you are, some
ninety miles away, you cannot have

these metaphors that mix like water and oil
in my own wrong practice (perhaps

Zen's single-hearted effort
lets you accept the ultimate *shin ku myo u*

that you are here, right now
(or, should I say, there). Unable to accept

things as they are, I sort papers, old cans
from the leaves, yet with care

not to sculpt the eddied, ochre mounds
as in raking. The rigid thought before

we act always leaves some trace, according
to Zen, whereas our own activity

should burn itself completely, leaving
no trace. I toss handfuls of leaves

high above my head, pressing moon-faced
Buddha for his calm and ordinary practice

Just Divine

You go to my head,
and you linger like a haunting refrain;
and I find you spinning round in my brain,
like the bubbles in a glass of champagne—
           Haven Gillespie

I don't want to leave any of that behind
—though it will take one wild divining rod
to dip the presence of these thoughts underground.
Living (or dying) without you near—willingly, but the ruminations!
Just what is it we get to keep? I plant these poems
in the primeval forest that you inhabit.
Other times we are at separate tables, separate counties.
I heard you on KQED at Moe's Books in Berkeley
with that terrific accent of yours, reading
about your 48th birthday in Jerusalem
and abortive rescues in high water
put to music, the American experience
you never thought you'd have.
And you are the American experience I'm having
that overtops the pines and birches of Flagstaff, Arizona.

Perfumed Girl on Foot

*after Ruth Orkin's photograph **American Girl in Italy, 1951***

My god, I'm outnumbered again on this street, where men have nothing better to do than whistle, jeer, or train their eyes on what they think is me. Did their mothers train *them* to hang around like frustrated jackals? I've seldom seen *women* who look this bored or dispossessed of industry. Most of these guys wouldn't deign to buy me dinner back home at Mama Leone's—yet they squander their minds in melancholic lust that frankly leaves me cold.

What if I were to go with one of them? Would his Italianate songs be any less static than those of some men I've been displeased to know? Let me walk through this menagerie without incident, without invective, without laughing in their bloody faces.

Finding It Out (I)

> *Ground the poem and do not have too many*
> *mysteries going on at once.*
>
> Paul Mariani

"What is it?" you ask the poet
in earnest, and now we, too,
want to know what (no, *how)* "bread
pudding of desire" means—as we mind
the fuddle of our own words, let alone desire.

And what is it, after all, our being here,
but a strong wish to be fed? Think, then,
of this workshop as a *bread riot.*
And as for you, how much reverence
can a great man take? (So what if education's
an ivory tower, I say, and hoist onto
his pedestal the next litterateur.)

How did I mean it, once like the irreverent
Lower East Side bully, seizing a Rhodes
scholar with "You are the first-
rate fellow striding the room,
your craggy words passageless"—
then robbing him of his Manhood
and making him a priest? Now
I'm trying hard
to think of a time when I wasn't ravenous
for the *pièce de résistance*
some scintillating tutor would offer
in his red-hot lectures. . .

As you read, your voice in the poems, husky,
sounds like desire—but no, it is instead
the priest's reverence for the word;
and you have given us use for it.

Finding it out: our own dark currents
traded for words, so that now,
your voice precisely fits us for desire.

III

Blindsided By Andrei Codrescu

I've never seen the man
and won't
and wouldn't
his radio voice
too potent
too strong
playful leviathan of words
publishing that leviathan
of books
sexy Romanian accent
thoroughly American man
this era's Nabokov
in operose achievement and genius
and today's essence of Beethoven
in language
context
dynamics
though even more audacious
in doing the crucial work
against expectation.

Yes—caught unprepared
as I read and listen
knowing
this writer is a prize
in my generation
and knowing furthermore
my own status
as an unashamed
sapiosexual.

Moments Finding Psychological Flow

> *It is the full involvement of flow*, rather than happiness,*
> *that makes for excellence in life.*
> Mihaly Csikszentmihalyi

- Exhilarations—what are they?
- What are the magical things?
- When a person is dying, is he primarily thinking or feeling?
- What have we done that makes others think we're odd (but find it delightful)?

Was that all it took in those days to wrest you away,
a big-eyed girl at a dance who made you stare
and stare by a fire in the cinder-fraught
air—you stared and I mused, is that all it takes?

Our bond flowed asymmetrically—
all things patterned after walking down tracks
across town to meet halfway in a blizzard, then tramping
the perimeter of town all day, like snow-borne
idiots. I said you were the only one I knew
who liked getting in the middle of what most
call inclement weather. Another day
in pelting hail we crossed tribal ground, discussing
Eiseley and Lopez. Difficult things flowed along.

If that's all it took, try going back before
our each-in-the-other, let struggle and play vanish,
words vaporize, then let you conceive how that's all it takes.

**flow: a sense of effortless action in a moment that strikes one as attaining the ultimate
exceptional experience*

Arguing With the Expert

Now about that novel, Syd Field tells me
in his highly acclaimed Screenplay: *The Foundations
of Screenwriting*, you must realize *character is action;
what a person **does** is who he is, not what he **says**.*
I want to tell him that in a novel about 1960s Alaska,
people *would* sit around talking, to the exclusion
of action. Their behavior *was* their dialogue then,
in the '60s—especially in Alaska.

But Syd knows all this; he's a veteran. (He's also
in Beverly Hills, and I need to talk to him.)
In one of his chapters, he wonders aloud
about the best way to turn any writing
into a screenplay—which, he allows, is not easy.

I want to take issue with Syd, pointing out the success
of French films like *My Night at Maud's* and *Claire's Knee*
—and America's *My Dinner With Andre*, where all the two men did
was eat and talk. And a certain niche audience ate it up.

But I have my own problems with this novel, begun at 17
some 40 years ago, since it seems that each time I pick it up,
I'm intruding in the characters' lives—perversely
curious and telling them what to say.
Obviously, they're on their own now; I see that.
Then there's the old fear of "Did I write that?
I don't remember saying that," further stressing
I'm just an interloper here.

Syd—my protagonist has a maroon MGA
and gatherings at his place where people
drink espresso, listen to jazz, and talk endlessly about Zen,
Schopenhauer, art, and Proust. They worship both
sound and silence—and major in philosophy for the fun of it.
Ergo, thinking is fun, and talking about thoughts is what they do.
Endlessly, Syd.

Getting It Right

after the prodigy of Kitty Robinson and a Jim Simmerman reading

She was so earnest, and so moonstruck:
What stalled in her mind as she roamed streets
with such resolve that I believed her motion had meaning?
Letting her lucid times construe all the rest,
I would bring sense to her forgetting
one instant in the next.

The grief of this lie is as heavy as hearing you
read in verse about the connectedness of all things,
how everything relates—demonically, almost.

The trouble this gives you
sets up networks of memory in me,
connections, remembering one who has lost
her power to hook up to anything for very long.

The staccato of your words comes at me like shrapnel;
leaving the room as you read is like refusing to cry.
Again I think of a woman whose steel-trap mind for precepts
misses daily connections. Yet for you, dear careful poet,
the sense lies in unfastening; the way you make it clear
ought to guarantee a model working of things
without, as you lament, "burning out the circuitry."

Things We Might Miss

> *Our shared life is not, after all, some story*
> *whose end I can keep rewriting.*
> Martha Cooley

We turned behind Arizona piñon, easing off the highway.
Above me on cinder road, you gyrated handsomely as the sun
punished your backside and your sweat rained on me. Much
whooshing of nearby cars made us fancy the disappearance
of our cover: dim figment for travelers—seeing *us* burn
up the road! Lying on our little heap of clothes,

I wondered how our urgency always seemed so close
to a leisurely saunter. We were on that highway
heading for the guitar repair shop, when we started to burn
vis-à-vis our dialogue. I had just called you "sonny"
in mimic of your college chum, whose grin once disappeared
when I let fall I wasn't your mom, but your great-aunt. Much

is made of *chronos*, no matter what you've heard. This much
is sure: For fine-tuned savvy, no one else comes close—
you're as ancient as the air. Years can disappear
in the unabashed oozing and trickling of sensation. Highways
vanish when language is a sultry flash flood and the sun's
heat is wild, yet quietly emphatic. Love can be borne.

It's funny how tension—the taut, expectant kind—will burn.
"Facts and truth," Faulkner said, "really don't have much
to do with each other." The facts are these: I have a son
your age. The cinder side road has been barricaded closed.
Once, in removing your wrist-brace beside a highway,
you forgot to return it to your strumming arm. Disappearing

cars across Hell Canyon didn't see us, so we disappeared.
You lost your wrist-brace that day. Maybe it burned,
or now it gathers snow. We loved "in the old high way
of love," as I believe Yeats said it for us, yet in much
the same way a wrist-brace is lost, or a door closed,
I lost you in a year's time to Zen. Or as the sun

finally disintegrates *anything* left too long in the sun.
You know the things we might miss can't disappear
completely. Yet one day you're holding someone close,
and the next, all you've got to show is a sunburn,
his poems, guitar tapes, the sun as witness and not much
else. Most of all, you figure on missing the way

new songs would issue from him, *sotto voce,* burning much
as from a sun-struck medium. The metaphors hit close
to home—highway songs so supernatural you knew he'd disappear.

On the Navajo Rez, 1985: Many Farms Dance

Tonight "Pals of Disco" are in full swing,
with colored lights and a revolving
silver ball that makes the grass look
as if it's gyrating. Only in the dark
the kids consent to dance. Most wear black,
their favorite garb, but it's not their color. . .
I say to another teacher it's a shame
we can't guess who's dancing with whom—
and how when *we* were kids we sure as heck
danced *with* each other—the only sanctioned
way to achieve intimacy, heh-heh.
One doesn't need a partner now
—sad note, since it's a heady
thing to have someone ask you
to dance. It *means* something.

The kids conduct themselves with decorum,
looking endearing and spoony. I glance at the mesa
and the ubiquitous stars, and thank all the gods
I'm not teaching in Paradise Valley.

Desert Postcards: Two Expurgated Scenes

Red Sky at Night

Knowing when the horse
is going to breakneck
across the pocked road would help
us leave the land as we found it. But
this carnage is part of what we find:
lost pets, sheepdogs, stallions, prairie
dogs. Here, animals are left
as they are, not touched
or moved on tribal ground. There's one
less coyote, and that moon—
eclipsed again by a season
of moribund sunsets.

Only Road Out of Town

Seeing the strewn carcasses in
various states of decay reminds
me of something a professor
told me last year: Cows have evolved,
and learned to manage cattle guards.
These and other livestock have jumped
only to be scythed, bludgeoned
or bounced to death.

Two men were driving the road
to Piñon at night when a mare crashed
into their windshield, rolled over
the top of the car, and continued
her gallop off into the night. All
were unscathed. I try hard to imagine cows
gingerly picking their way across grates.

Three Tragedies For the Art Teacher, 1985

I

Realizing that it is foolish to expect parity
in our zeal for one another, I nonetheless
flinch at your unstruck mien, your
practiced inertia, skilled otherness,
dry-eyes.

II

You may sashay through the vagaries
of your mind, frolic in Elysian Fields,
make passion your credo, but it was only parsley

III

Motus animi continuus,
the virile mind
won't slow, minds.

Winding It Up

In this house your words practice my mind, correct
as a metronome. I weep at words. This, others
suspect, is emotional lability. Would you worry
the ghosts and spectral rooms, as I have done—
feel the very air bullying you, shearing
away present walls and fine talk?

Outside, clouds sift calcium dust on waiting forms.
This light drape of snow, like your words, can't
last, won't mean much more than the infernal drip
of rivulets in the sun's fervor. . . In old photos
left in the car, your demon rustles the celluloid,
curling now like some tortured spiritual whorl.
I misplace fresh metaphors, and rush to snap open
fortune cookies; running through at least twenty-five,
I find no poetry, but plenty of missing articles:
"You will make change for better." Cookie bits
litter the ground like consolation prizes.

Love bothers us; what is there to do but fret
or poeticize? As if learning a language,
I conjugate each verb between us—
but none, not a word, hints
at termination. Then you do.

United

The misfortune of marriage is the proximity
of its fruit, its superabundance.
                    Søren Kierkegaard

In marriage, partners settle in
to something I don't like.
                    Marie Cox

Whenever you want to marry someone,
go have lunch with his ex-wife.
                    Shelley Winters

And further, Woody Allen tells us that "marriage is the death of hope." But what all this is *really* about is the absence of tension.

There just *has* to be that tautness with men and women—the kind that makes them anticipate. You know what I mean: the *desirable tension* between people that loses energy, turns flaccid, as they become accustomed. Keeping it there is the art—yet most seem slipshod in letting it go....

So you may want to ask beforehand: *Do you feel that tension when we're together?* Otherwise, on this typically solemn occasion, you may be stepping to Kierkegaard's malevolent tune of all matters handy, easy, and neat—and way too much of a good thing.

Chant Royal

However can I get her on her back? he mused.
Dear God, she intellectualizes everything. Just what
will move her to quit thinking? I want to see this thing fused
now—I've got a picture of my hands moving over her. It's not
that what we have already, what we say, doesn't excite me. Lord
knows, her voice is a rousing strip-tease. But when I move toward
her, she cringes like a cornered hare, her eyes in desperate furor
and prohibitive! I tell her then, "I'd like to know you in more
ways than through our poems and chats, and let things, too,
resonate with the body part...." She's going! Should I try humor?
"Lady, don't! Lie down—I want to talk to you."

She's wary. Amazing how I always get these reluctant ones, confused
about their sexuality, me, or how they got in this spot.
How CAN I get her on her back, without making her feel used?
(That seems to be their main complaint, even when they're so hot
I'm never enough.) Actually, I think women are dreadfully bored
by men's desires: always deficient in true regard and reduced to stored
sperm instead of tenderness. My wanting to have her on the floor
or plowing her atop this table, as Gauguin did it in *The Wolf at the Door*,
makes me churlish and indelicate. No matter the plan, she'll think me too
peremptory. Her words as I drift bedwards settle it—temptress? or
lady? "Don't lie down! I want to talk to you."

She wants to talk to me. Just talk. I swear, I'm not used
to waiting this long for something physical. How many sonnets have I got
to write before she lets me "act out the rest," as Donne rapped while he perused
some lovely's physiognomy? And how often has she said she's not
buying the body-mind dichotomy? (If that's the case, one word
leading to another should have a corollary in the bedroom.) Sure, I've heard
the virtues of waiting, leading-up-to, teasing—all the ploys of the whore;
but this one's had practice of a different kind. She's more
inviting than she wants to be, or knows. "What should I do,"
I ask her, "die for want of you?" She smiles. "Would you cajole this poor
lady? Don't lie. Down! I want to talk. To you."

I've been reading to her for hours. And it's kind of nice, amused
both of us, actually. If I was trying to get her in the sack, I forgot
why, since words are more provocative than I'd guessed. Oh, I've abused
the notion of intimacy before, feeling foolish after the sex was shot.
Right now I've got a good feel of her sense of life, and a general disregard
for, say, her breasts, although she'd find it devilishly hard
keeping them out of my face. I keep thinking what we've got in store
for each other. What is that perfume? Gardenia? Lilac? I'm more
desperate than I've ever been, and she knows it. What I want to do
with her defies words. "Please, no more questions. And don't be sore,
lady. Don't. Lie down. I want to. *Talk?* To you,

I suppose I'm some sort of intellectual release. In lieu of sex, you choose
a fine idea. You're telling me that somewhere along the way, brains begot
pleasure. Now tell me how long you'll keep a man at arm's length. And who's
going to believe we had this conversation?" —I can see I have a lot
at stake: my reputation, pride, credibility. Without a single word
I wanted *her*. Instead, she's had *her* way with *me*, stirred
things up philosophically. Now, is a certain tension more
alluring than the crashing together of bodies (and letting passion make poor
our desire)? Passion. What's passion? Ladies will construe
it in cerebral patter. Let them. What follows is détente. "Sure,
lady. Don't lie down. I want to talk to you."

Envoi

Men, realize when they talk, it makes you want them more;
their resistance makes you crave it in a closet, on the floor.
Eventually. Don't try to tell them what to do.
Be patient, not grasping. Here's what you must say when your
ladies don't lie down: "I want to talk to you."

You See

what our words are,
after all—paroxysms
of the hottest desire; how love
transmutes; encoded murmurs.

When I say
desire it's not
that clichéd bit.
Not anything you've
heard before. Not sex.
Not fond regard. Enough
to say that intercourse
of the sensual kind
would overstate our case.

Although I could lie
beside you for hours,
quite still, or rolling over
and over verdant knolls,
grassy and prolix,
your hardness unraveling
the paradox of which I speak.
Yes—intercourse would be
too much. Or not enough.

Book Signing: Poems

No sale here today, or perhaps
in the microcosm *ever*—not even
with Peter Sellers' outrageous
photo on the cover featuring
Sinead Cusack's knees. But stopping
by my table, though, are two who say
they wrote a kind of poesy years back—
a physician whose master's thesis probed
the juncture of verse and medicine, and the jocund
chap who says he shot away from writing
but regrets it and now wears a cap
boldly lettered NRA. To him I suggested
he get fired up in a free-for-seniors
writing class, and also to him I gave
a copy of my book gratis. Another man talked
for an hour over my books about auras,
the benefits of reverse-osmosis-treated
water, and the saving of a woman's life
by a doctor's bedside manner—
his Mr. Hyde changing to Dr. Jekyll
just in time. My next book signing
will be on the Grand Canyon Skywalk,
where the author will have more leverage.

1960s Marvels

Upchucking each morning
as guinea pigs
for Enovid-E
we wonder if parturition
can be any worse
than this.

We intrepid marvels
are outdoing ourselves
with this regimen,
nauseated and in sync
with the gutsy pediatrician
placing *Stop* at *Two* brochures
in his waiting room.

IV

With Ridiculous Caution

On southeast Georgia farmland, on a road that runs
to mire in March rains, near no thing
human, abrupts a stranded graveyard. There is no church
for miles. This is a cemetery for travelers,
where manifest destiny brought some of them to lie down
and sleep out the rest of their crossing.

Once I found this hushed community I returned often, walking
the ground so many times I memorized their names. Diphtheria moved
through their young like gossip among tattlers,
like fatal slander. Wives outlived their men by ten years,
at least; husbands followed wives within only two.
The crude stones, some unmarked, held names and dates
imprecisely scrawled by makeshift tool: Bennett, Thornburgh,
Strom, Taylor, Booker, Sims, Johnson, Albright. But some stones
only *seemed* blank; their indented surfaces could be revealed
by a method known to the art's cognoscenti as "rubbings."
People have traveled cemeteries all over a country, gathering
anthropological scraps from the process.

My presence in this burial place is the old maid's foolish
anticipation. . .those lying about are at a loss for words, and getting
to know them is like listening for the cat with no bell.
Al, the savvy southern boy, has dared me to find
the Parkerville Cemetery; I have spent the day to win
this dare. Since then, the dead ones and I have exchanged
theories on meaning. This small wood has escaped
the insidious secret of Spanish moss—that decadent drape
on trees holding *chiggers* in swarms.

Absurdly careful, I begin to gentle the letters on stones
onto rice paper with a charcoal stick, remembering those
back at the office worrying, "It's funny she's so keen
on finding that cemetery." It is funny, that finding
some of the dates on stones, I had to find them all, since
not knowing means I would have to lie down here forever
to unriddle these truncated lives.

How do we call death? —"passing," as these souls were when their bodies
became as useless as destinations: *motus animi continuus.*

Sun slants through trees, layering my face;
the wind rubs across it, yielding nothing,
nothing but texture. I struggle to lift a toppled
half-stone of graveness: infant mortality.
Some children's graves are diagonal bricks
in circles of leaves, nothing more.

Slip

A simple matter of bothering
    the balance
that keeps one sane:
It's a wrench—a tipping of oxygen,
a spill of quintessential glucose;
and you, in stuporlike calm, hoping
to finesse the realm of measured thought,
of balanced blood.

Looking at Rorschachs, Then at Walls

At night as I languish with Sappho
the space around her words becomes
more prominent than the poems themselves—

It's the way it is when voices in a room fade
down and out and your own heartbeat grows louder
or when everyone else recedes and the well-lit
room expands in an aura of heat and light,
or in giving birth, when that moment of greatest pressure
outdoes pain that rightly should persist.

Who's to know at these times what should be far,
and at the foreground? Late at night as I read,
the sounds of lovers plow through these walls, beating
down a faint erudition; her worsening cough
says he lets her sleep less and less.
The poems I read run to white heat;
looking too long at the page will do that.
I know that the voice of those words, like the boy
poised over his companion next door, is unstoppable.

Once in school when asked to attend to the shapes
of ink blots for their meaning, we stared at them *instead*,
closed our eyes for the negative prints, then opened them
to fix the images on walls. Why we did this, instead,
is unclear; only that focusing on form was less troubling
to fourteen-year-olds than looking for content.

Now as the business of form and content shifts, overturns
like lovers, gauche in their quick want, so as to make
the two tantamount, words on the page resume
force, take on their full coloration, augment,
in a flood tide of lettering.

In the Field

On our hands and knees, scrambling
for beads and the antiquity
of our own tradition:
Just how much distance can one take?

Dear, the lessons I could learn
in this position—ritual advance
and retreat, precursor of sex,
telescoped views, surrender
for once and all of hubris.

Shards lie scattered like pieced
repetitions of words, symbols
of our own primitive
and tricky distance. You sketch
the site while my mind sketches your love
of context. In the field our words
winnow what is hard
and bright from the rubble.

On the ride back, dialectics steer
us who have now gone mad
for provocation. . .I question you then,
relentless as a tutor in his hard
pitiless way. Is this how it can happen?

Rhodes Scholar (*Picaro*)

And when hee hath the kernell eate,
Who doth not fling away the shell?
John Donne

You are always the first-rate fellow
striding the room, professing,

your craggy words passageless,
mind's bastion. You don't even know

how to drive a car. You once chopped
off your fingertip with a paper-

cutter. You let the more exotic girls
drive you home, to town and airports.

You womanized each term like a man
gone mad for miscellany. The girls

found out about each other, and wrote
you a letter signed by all three.

One of them made a cake for the man
whose professional life was above

reproach, whose birthday was the day
after St. Valentine's: a debit-red cake

iced white, decorated with two whole
confectionized measures of your bassoon

sonata. You held court at intermissions
and wowed them at concerts;

at home you lied to the ladies,
while fearless and sound in *Who's Who.*

She Finds He Is Standing Before Her

after Yeats

Those words, no token of your pause,
Sung out counter to your standing there:
Poor surrogate words, at odds
With the stuff of eye-beams,
The real affair.

A Chastisement for John Donne

So, if I dreame I have you, I have you,
for all our joyes are but fantasticall.
                    Elegie X, "The Dreame"

Yet, love and hate mee too....
                    "The Prohibition"

I want to despise you,
that your wife
died upon birth
of her twelfth child.
But I can only
marvel, instead,
at your conceits.

Was it your con-
ceit that awed
her so? Was it
that which held
her down, "love-
slain," caught in a
feminine compromise?

Did it help you write
that she, with child
nearly every
year, held
her tongue and
let you love,
let it all happen?

O John.
The paradox of
this death
staggers your own
metaphysics. It's
"owner bee

of thee one hour"
murdered in
her bed. Dear Anne!

When death lifted
her last child
from arms that seemed
never to abstain
from yours, she canon-
ized herself,
and left you to
realize
that even the best
Petrarchan conceit
can only play,
and love, among words.

Redaction for Jim Simmerman

I'm trying to think
how this life
drove you to end yours
as poet, teacher,
wry observer who once said
in a poem, "Nothing good lasts."

Another hip replacement
was ahead, your dog died,
girlfriend left—
all counterbalanced
by the awards,
karate black belt,
admiring students,
published poems.

Still, how could you?
What antidotes
to your head games
could anyone have presumed
to offer? In some needling way
I must know why you couldn't look
farther ahead. Just a *few days*
might have done it: the paradigm shift,
an unjaded look at things, the next book
and reading, the new dog, the new girl,
your students' esteem
and homage of colleagues—
all these that could have made you
look again. Just a few days more,
to stop the gun at your head.

Dead Air

For him momentum
is the succession
of cued-up sides,
the glossy spin
of black vinyl
deftly slid
from its case,
and always on time

he knows when he opens
the mic
he can't use the words
he wants—
digital countdown
won't permit Roget
his paroxysm
takes too long

stand by
for the first time
ever he can't
go on
like this,
slumped over the board
with Tchaikovsky's *First*
and a Schubert trio
cued
and no one else
actually standing by
but the duffer
calling in
wanting like hell
to get on

Finding It Out (II)

Leaving your room
I realized that the rest
of the building had,
for an hour, dropped us
in glacial fashion, our iceberg
carrying us out to sea. Icebergs in Arizona.
Yes. Our dialogue back to back
on that ice floe showed me just how long it is
one can be hidebound
before a shocking sensation,
like ice loosening, occurs.
How could anyone have intervened?
What could they, themselves disenfranchised
of the pleasure of formality breaking down
and slipping away like so much
melting resolve, have done?

It's at these times one expects
to stutter; yet we moved, still back to back,
with the current—everything we said crystalline
and hard and transfusing the seven-eighths
of our words still submerged.

Does the renegade ice mass feel its precise
point of departure? When we talked of writing,
where were we going? This much is clear:
We headed out so far that no one
came looking—and stayed intact, managing
to gentle some of our own flood's tide.

Finding it out: our own dark currents
traded for words so that now,
hearing your voice, I break.

On the Road

What comes is not to be avoided
What goes is not to be followed
           Master Daibai

That's the trouble with love. People think it involves rights.
           Philip Wylie, *Tomorrow!*

You will still see the sky
in common—companionate—
belt of Orion
gibbous moon
quavering stars
you can't go too far
for me to keep loving
the roomy expanse
between us. I adore a good oxymoron,
like *bittersweet* or *loathsome charm* or Shakespeare's
"heavy lightness." Neither will I look for you
nor you present yourself.
Keep going. I won't see you
anytime soon. Or at all.

Screed

How young you are, and cunning as false dawn—
love still as spurious as I thought it was;
words from priests were not more eloquent. This does
us both disservice. When light wanes, you pawn
the blackguard in you, serving up your love
as stars, tokens, confidences, vows.
Once, thrusting us out of a light that grows
dark side's eclipse, moon-blind as you drove
us awry, you drowned the stars, capsized my heart.
Your love is like some ring around the moon,
untouching, airy, all-for-wishing light—
your mind, a rococo impostor, gilt-edged art.
You're like a shirt that's caught mid-way, too soon,
over head: light's smothering, unprepared false night.

Precipitate Harvest

It was his mind: calling-card
of poetry, forever catching me
like a farm girl, off guard
and chastened for propensity

of always naming things. And yet, before
the posturing and second-thinking start,
love cultivates the finest clearings; or
words are velveteen before the vault

from furrowed mind to touch.
Speculate on the spring of abstract love,
how consummation wants too soon and much
to pluck taut shoots from the excited grove.

The Sap Begins to Circulate

One day, I was already old, in the entrance
of a public place, a man came up to me.
                    Marguerite Duras

Here we are, alone again.
                    Louise-Ferdinand Celine

A woman aging ordinarily,
I contemplate your coming
to me, coming
into me like a man might
slip into earth's warm loam
or dive into the recesses of intellect.
Either one, your entry changes
the way I age, now a spectacular
trip over the hill and through your woods.

V

Descant

I wish I'd been
in your class
I *am* in your class
you are my tutor
back of beyond
since classrooms
don't allow a respectable
distance. Respect fades
in obliged nearness
into a sort of stupor

Someone is speaking in sonorous
tones about Jesus, James, and John
but this is the library
genealogy room
and no matter how splendidly
said (ostensibly to draw
others in), the spiel doesn't help
my own silent reading
of Wm. James' *Pragmatism*,
so I'm getting out of here

Passing Over

One never comes again to the same.
Osho

You, who I have decided
are my last intrigue,
have transcended the whole scene.
The dialogue, your *gemütlichkeit,*
galvanized a passel of poems
and let loose the fillip to eroticism
flourishing at a distance. Even now
your words are packing a punch somewhere
I can't hear. Yet for moments that refuse
forgetting, as Nani schooled Osho,
"never ask for more. What is, is enough."

Rarámuri

Father Juan Fonte, Society
of Jesus, stepped into
1600s Mexico, its *barrancas*,
and saw men who could run
deer to exhaustion. They must
have God, he thought. Give them God.
The Jesuits' gifts of goats, fruit trees,
metal tools failed to wrest an unbroken
song from the *Rarámuri*, who kept
their *tesgüinada*, music, scattered fields,
but shrewdly welcomed the god-foil
to sorcery.

Now, the *matachines* dance
with the *dutuburi*, mingling of God
with gentile. How long?
How long can you outrun, keep
your planting-stick? In this chronicle
of retreat, only the Jesuits kept plumbing.
Well, God is persistent.

In your sprint against all time, will
the Chihuahua al Pacifico race **you**
to exhaustion? Can reed flute, rattle, violin
counter what is circling you
in absurd overrefinement?

Father Fonte and his padres
could learn this from their proselytes:
that your nuptial with the land was a shotgun wedding.

And it wasn't the fiestas that rankled
in the Jesuits' minds—in men who cultivate
austerity like a lover; it was the *tesgüino*,
mild, sacred beer from corn—sole
deliverance from cave, austerity.

Your children die to become stars;
death is a land of opposites, where souls
move in moon's day—homage paid backwards

by the living, left-hand, sidelong. You have
no counterpart. No Third-World tryst awaits
men whose poetry is in the running,
and no mere diastolic measure says it all:
You have run 200 miles without stopping,
400 years steadfast.

All But the Mist

He lifted the receiver, then put it down again
in much the same way a man would lower a gun
from his temple on second thought. Could he stand
calling someone (much less being found dead)
in a room this many shades of blue? The mist
from his recent shower was all, indeed, that was *not*
blue, settling on the room's several mirrors.

His truck had broken down next to the state prison,
and now he was incarcerated in this motel room
which could take a prize for the most blue kitsch
in a space the size of a small gazebo. Would anyone
on the other end of a phone sense his disquietude,
his impulse to laugh? He wanted desperately
to exercise his right to make a single phone call.
He would call this woman who had found him
on the back of his latest book—36 years
after their steady stream of notes passed in study hall.

~

She had made reservations to stay in the blue-hued motel
he'd called her from months ago. Perhaps the Iranian couple
at the front desk now wondered why she requested Number 14.
If they asked, she would tell them without rhapsodizing. They
didn't.

Yet coming to this room with its blue furor of detail,
she knew she would not spend even a moment in it
with him. She thought an ephemeral mist encircled her,
but it gave way to only thinking it so. And she had to be done
with contemplation—something useful instead,
that which was useful. Even now, she was neglecting
something, but was unsure what it was. Lying on the bed,
she determined, as surely as she breathed the excogitated
mist, that as she had entered the room by herself,
she would leave it taking him with her.

Long Shot

Today by happenstance at a Tucson gas station I saw a man
—now a writer/historian—from our history of passing reckless
billets-doux in study hall

At the moment he looked into her face
and closed the years, he let his hand
drop that was already searching
for another cigarette, and returned her stare.
All their recent missives, the phone calls
and an ongoing speculation did not help this moment.
And he did not help her either, but stood there, waiting.
She knew she could not now expect a *deus ex machina*
bearing her self-possession. But she wanted to stay like this, looking
at him in just this way. Before she got into her car she smiled at him
as one would before an embrace.

Renaissance Man in a Secular Place

Going home is like visiting a shrine of your own juvenilia:
What is it that keeps things transfixed,
like a camera's stop-action or a runner become bronze?
You know the leaves are new, and the wind and sunbreak ancient.

What is it that keeps things transfixed?
For the man at the bar the judgment is foregone;
you know the leaves are new and the wind and sunbreak ancient,
but he curses the cold—it's "painful."

For the man at the bar, the judgment is foregone.
No longer the affable gent of your seminar,
he curses the cold. It's painful
watching Scotch work its waywardness on him.

No longer the affable gent who seeks
a difference of opinion—now there's a critical air.
Watching the Scotch work its waywardness on him,
you wish he'd go home. He has the kindest eyes....

Difference of opinion, essential to air, is
his classroom stock-in-trade, all-electric dialogue.
You wish he'd go home. He had the kindest eyes,
telling you his need to see those he loves in discovery.

His classroom stock-in-trade: all-electric dialogue,
a requirement for him that *hurts* in its urgency.
Telling you his need to see those he loves in discovery,
he speaks of the wife he loved, discovering—someone else.

The requirement for him that hurts is transfixed,
like a camera's stop-action or a runner become bronze;
difference, Scotch-skewed, estranges now. He won't go home—
Going home is like visiting a shrine of your own juvenilia.

Fable for J. S.

. . .all are subject to time and mischance.
Ecclesiastes 9:11

The wind blows wherever it pleases. You hear its sound,
but you cannot tell where it comes from or where it is going.
John 3:8

Your smiling recalls for me
Arthur Lemon's *The Wooing of Daphnis*:
She leans languidly against a sitting bull
while Chloe stares her helpless from the grass,
his eyes tugging.

Your smile staggers the squall blustering
in your head. There's stuff in that smile
to run right over "nothing good lasts." Listen—
I'd charge a toll to keep that smile maintained,
to see the élan whizz from your lips to your eyes.

Now we're at your eyes. I'm looking
for a metaphor for eyes—even a mixed one will do.
Something like: you, sitting with your head in your hands
and your eyes on the floor—or your eyes
scuffing through leaves, perhaps.

Do you know what I'm saying? Let's just say
The Wooing of Daphnis and that grin of yours
are more believable than your despair. Helpless
at times, I have learned from your smile
in my fashion, from riot to resurrection.

Idée Fixe, Alaska

At night, we'd watch the fluttering Northern Lights—
sinuous, like ribbons, they used to say,
yet a sight too strong for any known simile.
Beyond all renderings in words, these nights:
nights that long could occupy a man
in drink that loosed his mind—never mind
a sky chromatic-streaked; a man could blind
himself by day in untilled snow, which ran
with sky lights all the way to Idaho.
Knaves, eccentrics, fugitives—their trick
was to escape to such a place and settle low,
whipping in and out of view, like arctic
lights: Just say this nighttime flickering show
preoccupies man's tendency to mimic.

Mother Leaving

"Just get my mother back safely to Austin,"
I said, "and next to Daddy, as she planned.
No funeral there." Later, putting on
your fleece coat, I reached inside a pocket,
my hand closing around stiff paper—
the half-stick of your favorite gum
in its orange wrapper. You seemed so recent then.
Searching the opposite side, I found
the crumpled foil wrapper holding
your used gum. It was as if your going
was a lie. It made me think of how
we're always sorting—prepared
to discard some things, saving others
as if they couldn't disappear.

Like So Many Sparks

From my bed in the darkened
room I see a red dot
and a white dot of light.
A flip of the switch
usually does it, but some things
can't be turned off.
That red dot warns that sparks
and smoke go hand in hand. Yet
it and the light that seeps
from the door's peephole
can mean only one thing:
there is no true ebony.

Think of it:
neon, headlights, clocks' dials,
street lamps, fireflies, stars,
moon, false dawn—
some things can't be turned off.
Even my mind dreams furiously illuminated.

Some things you don't
want to turn off. Like the banter
that flashes a splendid arc
of language-cum-longing, or like
the glint off nickel keys
in a concert hall.

There was a reflection of us, each
in the other, but saying what happened
would be like explaining how the moon
looks larger, more lambent, on the horizon.

A man needs advice in a newspaper
column: His concern is that when
he's in a dark room and starts
to cough, sparks fly from his mouth.
Between the sparks and the dark

is another thing. Spend the rest
of your nights trying to guess it.

The Sex We Talk

It's always been this way. Even when
you thought we spoke of reason, art,
or politics, we were already in that car,
pulling the walls in closer,
breathing hard and that's all,
but wasn't that enough—

talking issues that those stars
five miles out of town saw were really
sex. Or remember us on hands and knees
in classic pose to find what's missing—
and having a profusion of beads reflect
what we missed before we were this close
to the ground and each other.

—Talk so close to sex that your vehemence
in our chats made me want to give you photos
of my breasts, making you the voyeur
for your hot words alone. How fervent we are
when we speak. It's the thrashing about
of our minds that does it for us—since
like the operatic tenor and soprano
all we've done is sing to each other.

It has always seemed to me the variety of speech
(unlike that other intercourse) is endless.
Just keep talking. Or say nothing and continue to wait.

Please Refrain From Walking on the Bare Earth Until the Grass Has Been Born

A woman is so bollixed that she throws
her family's clothes out the window, thinking
it's time again to move. Passersby
eyeing the event think the clothes
are being discarded, and rush to claim
their outfits for the coming week.
The woman has moved eleven times
in the last year, and thinks she might
prefer being a streetwalker to being
married, so she could become established
and live in one place. Why stay
with these gypsies? Her yard is dotted
with KEEP OFF THE GRASS signs that seem
to draw people like a sideshow to tramp
in perverse circles on the bare earth.
Grass takes time, she thinks, like thought
and love. Her mind flutters to times
when boys called on her for proms and drives
in the constant countryside. Once a sandy-
haired boy with superior intelligence
stood her up for a dance, then sent roses
the next day. Once, she remembers, clover
abounded in untrammeled grass, as expansive
as today's trounced and worthless blacktop.
She watches nearly a dozen people
sorting through the impassive, lackluster
clothes as if at a 10-minute-limit bargain
table, and smiles at the dog worrying
one sock. He snarls in mock ferocity,
dragging her mind, too, down the cleft
sidewalk away from a crowd
whose only sound is the pounding of feet.

Missing Person

> *...as long as you wish*
> Sappho, *Fragment No. 45*

> *...I want*
> *...to hold*
> Sappho, *Fragment No. 76*

How I want you
to stay where you are
this aphrodisiacal frenzy
of mine
isn't going anywhere
this isn't *froideur*
there's a coziness about it
nice to hold
but I've got me
where I want me
as long as I wish

Where Did They Go?

There's something else
but I don't know what it is
we close our eyes
and can almost see
and hear what's Other
doesn't seem benevolent
just busy like us

There's something else
it's vibrating
it won't show itself
fully it will always be
unintelligible
neutral
just as the mirror at home
encompasses something else
besides resemblance
but we don't know what it is
we aren't looking hard enough

Mater

She had miscarriages
before and after me,
so I could have been
one of them. Instead
of the writer I am.
If she hadn't been
in the business of marriage,
she could have been
the artist she was.
Her sketches on every
paper surface remind me
of how dismally I've taken
her absence: The humor, the confidence
closed off now for good.
Grief, says the counselor,
is a spiral pulling down hard
to reverse. Someone
in this godawful protracted
quiet must be listening,
must be sentient.

The Sun is My Enemy

The title of this poem
is really the name
of a book I'm writing
about the inescapable
quality of hot weather
and how it heats
up our bodies
like the meat that they are
how we can't divest
ourselves of enough clothes
but can do the obverse
in winter,
the best, most healthful
season of all. Heatstroke
as a child killed
my tolerance for unmitigated
warmth. In summer, steep
teabags in *cold* water.

Dropping the Past

makes a light ringing sound
or shatter, like the fragments of shards.
"In fifty years it won't matter
a whit to those distant relations
after us," said a man in the laundromat—
the photos, trinkets, films, histories,
the accoutrements of our lives will,
as kindred memories fail,
all lose their allusions
and import and *raison d'etre*
and so will we.
Preposterous, really, to save
what we value where we live.
Better to leave words
that the anxious-to-dispose
heirs can't understand
but also can't do away with
or even think to look for
on a library shelf
with a friend
or in a fine bookstore
you used to frequent.

Felo-de-se

Is a riddle solved by the fact that I survive forever?
Is this eternal life not as enigmatic as our present one?
Ludwig Wittgenstein

Stop pity-
ing them. Some
who take their lives
are through.
They've finished
what it is they
came to do.
They're out of time
and glad
about
it. Some
are unattached
(not really mad)
and, unlike you,
have no remorse.
Let them go.
Let them. Let others
cluck-cluck-
cluck, "Of course."
Then let
your own
mere breath be
unaccustomed life.

Life Outside the Garden

Because we consume our resources at a destructive rate. . .
the imperatives remaining are two: to learn to share
and preserve, and to practice a "morality of scarcity."
Dr. William G. Pollard, Physicist,
Oak Ridge Laboratory, 1969

"If the current administration has its way, we'll be back in
business in no time!"
Cartoon caption c. 1970 for two sleazy men
hanging a shingle for backstreet abortion

The night my father got me his mind was not on me.
A.E. Housman

Babies bloom like oleander along a California freeway, while people carry placards to save prefetuses. Their graphics stagger those who think about abuse and neglect, orphans and starvation. Just how lucky is the fetus who lives to afford therapy for the inconvenience passed from mother to child? People with placards should interview fetuses that can talk back: the result of an abortion that was *not* performed 20, 30, or 40 years ago—then decide whether all fetuses are *valued* in a country where 70% of all pregnancies are unplanned. How is it ever right for a human to be the result of a blown condom or an extra drink?

"Garden of Eden Era Believed Nearing End," a headline proclaims, because in 1830 there were one billion people; in 1970, three and one-half billion. (You may fill in current numbers as you read this poem.) For those hoping to sail inky waters into yet another galaxy—fleeing our own quaint population cancer—know this: In the light years required to travel to a habitable planet, the ship would be overpopulated before you could arrive.

Meanwhile, what's needed here is a poem, not a tract: "Babies bloom...." I think of the California pediatrician who swore he had *too much* business: "We don't care that some don't believe in birth control— they don't have to copulate at all! Far too many think they're virtuous enough if they teach their six kids not to toss beer cans."

Hunger Flight

Three cashiers chased frantically out
into the friendly store's parking lot,
as if to save someone felled
by stroke or runaway car. Soon
they marched a woman and her two small lads
with widening eyes back
into the clotting groups of shoppers
waiting for an altogether different kind
of report. Behind the mother
(who stood reed-straight), a dark-haired boy
pushed the store's cart, straining
with its red-handed load of beans
and pasta, lettuce, fruit, meat
and that commodity we are told
Jean Valjean risked everything for.

Verbum Sat Sapienti

> *There is something naked about eyes; they*
> *...have never really learned to dissimulate....*
> John Fowles

But *yours* are a backstair;
waiting, constrained, they allow nothing—
subdued, then: not cold, just not saying.
You, distracted in the quiet
systematism that causes you to be,
to do, to decline to say,
are, like your eyes, ordered
(the shapes of laws, postulates,
proximate causes);

I cannot regard you,
just poorly calculate.

Ever After

In his poem "The Afterlife," Billy Collins tells us
that "everyone is right, as it turns out. You go
to the place you always thought you would go...."
And let's face it, everyone is curious about what's next.

A day before Mother died, with two
of her daughters close by, we saw her eyes
scan from side to side across the wall.
"What do you see, Mother?" asked her youngest.
"The Apostles," she answered—and this from a woman
whose mind stayed lucid to the penultimate moment.
So if my mother—raised a Tyson—said she saw the Apostles
(and if Billy is right), she probably did.

Where (I, as a Mark Twain agnostic-atheist, ask) *does*
the energy go? Why is the sense of hearing the last one
to leave? All I know is it takes some EMDR
and two years with a grief guide versed in the precepts
of Zen to arrest the least prepared of us.

Reunion Koan

One world at a time.
                              Thoreau

Children, one earthly Thing truly experienced,
even once, is enough for a lifetime.
                              Rilke

One real world is enough.
                              Santayana

It must be, since it took only one
to make the circle back into yours.
Once seems enough for nearly everything:
one child, one published book, one nuptial tie—
and surely, once to take your hand in greeting
must be that earthly Thing. For me it is enough.
"Must it be?" asked Beethoven, then added, "It must be."

Draw a Parallel

I let go your hand, but never
the ambiguities, which catch
me up in their deep, convoluted
hearts. It comes down to this:
Like some exotic kinship,
our yearning moves us over
each other in affectionate
and pristine discovery; or consider
wanton hands traveling
the coolest of restraint.
Lineage not of blood,
but that descent
from a tradition of lovers celebrating
a common and optimum distance.

Loners

 are in peril, realize—
easy prey for misfits
with guns
or without.
There is no refuge
in seclusion:
the hermitry
is magnetized
for exploitation.
Ergo, live among throngs
whose clamor
you can't abide,
or in privacy
whose splendor
has no hope of rescue,
if it comes to that.

On the Foyer Wall

In a black and white still,
a man holds his drink in both hands
like a sullied flower

and sits, gazing at a woman's knees.
Her short skirt, made shorter
as she sits, is hiked up mid-thigh.

Peter Sellers is *Hoffman*
in a sleeper about a low-key, odd joe
who blackmails a bride-to-be

into spending the weekend with him.
In this congealed moment, his eyes
are rapacious, but breeding and decorum

keep him transfixed like a Phrygian king
up to his chin in water, thirst unslaked.
He will not move. Even if

this man (the actor whose heart
in real life "just faded away")
were alive, he might always stay

in this posture of leaning and staring.
Although it would take only the remove
of one hand from his glass to her knee

(which is as close to him as his own knee),
he will not touch her. If her knee
were bronze he would not handle it.

His eyes have that fine mingling of lust
and embarrassed constraint. He will not
reach out. His adamantine gaze is fixed

in just that opiate instant
before he or she must speak. He leans
without touching, the unpronunciations

on his lips always ready to obtain.
The virtual grapes are within
his reach, if only he could make a start.

If the camera were to roll past this dopey
moment, would motion make him sorry?
Can you say for certain that he,

or Tantalus, would want to realize
the grave high rhythms or the maddening
counterpoint of the next moment?

Megathrust Exit

Your *first motion*
a *fall* in tidal wave lingo,
you take everything
with you
in a leading-depression
wave. Fast-ebbing—
it's a disaster
of a trough,
of a long-lived drawdown:
teletsunami, *mon ami.*

Notes

"Mantle" was written 20 years after the upheaval—without the least dulling of memory or sensation. The five-minute earthquake, comprising widespread vertical and horizontal displacements, was rated a 9.2 event on the moment magnitude scale, earlier measured 8.5 on the Richter scale.

In "Maple Leaves and Moon," the Japanese phrase *shin-ku-myo-u* refers to the Zen Buddhist principle that true being comes out of nothingness, minute-to-minute, and it is translated "from true emptiness, wondrous being."

"Mother Leaving," "Mater," and "Ever After" are in memory of Johnnye Cox.

"Chant Royal" is a formulaic improvisation in the opposite gender on a clichéd male pickup line that has become a parody of itself.

In "On the Navajo Rez," Many Farms is a Bureau of Indian Affairs high school in northern Arizona, where the author taught English in the 1980s and again in the 1990s, before pressing on to college instruction.

"Rarámuri" ("foot-runners") is the name that the Tarahumara Indians living in Copper Canyon, Mexico, prefer. Barefoot or in homemade sandals, they can outrun deer in serpentine canyons.

"Please Refrain From Walking on the Bare Earth..." took its name from the most effective and lyrical sign of its kind at Arizona State College, Flagstaff, in 1965.

My thanks to the editors of the following publications in which these poems, or versions thereof, have appeared:

Several poems appeared in chapbooks *With Ridiculous Caution* (2013) and *O, But in the Library* (2017), published by Finishing Line Press.

Seems: "Sestina *Pro Tempore*." (Copyright © 2002 by Karl Elder, Editor. First appeared in Seems No. 35, 2002, and nominated for a Pushcart Prize by Karl Elder. Reprinted by permission of the Editor.)

The George Wright Forum: A Journal of Cultural and Natural Parks and Reserves: "With Ridiculous Caution." (Copyright © 1994 by The George Wright Society, Inc. First appeared in *The George Wright Forum*, Vol. 11, No. 2, 1994. Reprinted by permission of the Editors and in the Prescott National Forest *Granite Tablet* in 1994.)

Voices on the Wind: "1960s Marvels," "About Desire," "A Chastisement for John Donne," "All But the Mist," "And That's Final," "Arguing With the Expert," "Before It Gets There: The End of Postmortem Blues," "Blindsided by Andrei Codrescu," "Book Signing: Poems," "Building It Up," "Chant Royal," "Dead Air," "Desert Postcards: Two Expurgated Scenes," "Draw a Parallel," "Dropping the Past," "Ever After," "Fable for J.S.," *"Felo-de-se,"* "Finding It Out (I)," "Finding It Out (II)," "For the Concrete Man," "Getting It Right," "Hazard," "Hunger Flight," *"Idée Fixe*, Alaska," "Immersion," "In the Field," "Its Own Magic," "Just Divine," "Life Outside the Garden," "Like So Many Sparks," "Loners," "Long Shot," "Looking at Rorschachs, Then at Walls," "Maple Leaves and Moon," "Mantle," "Megathrust Exit," "Men in Bars," "Mindfulness," "Moments Finding Psychological Flow," "Mother Leaving," *"Ne Plus Ultra,"* "On the Foyer Wall," "On the Navajo Rez, 1985: Many Farms Dance," "On the Road," "Perfumed Girl on Foot," "Please Refrain From Walking On the Bare Earth Until the Grass Has Been Born," "Precipitate Harvest," "Renaissance Man in a Secular Place," "Reunion Koan," "Rhodes Scholar (*Picaro*)," "Screed," "Slip," "She Finds He Is Standing Before Her," "Spanning," "Study in Yellow: Above Hell Canyon," "The Sap Begins to Circulate," "The Sex We Talk," "The Sun Is My Enemy," "Subliminal: No Waiting Ever," "Things We Might Miss," "Three Tragedies For the Art Teacher, 1985," "United," "Where Did They Go?" "Winding It Up," "You See," and "You, Somewhere." Reprinted by permission of the Editor.

National Federation of State Poetry Societies 1992 Contest Magazine: "Rarámuri."

Agnes Scott College *1984 Writers' Festival Magazine:* "Verbum Sat Sapienti"

After earning a bachelor's in comparative literature at the University of Redlands, **Susan Stevens** studied for her master's in creative writing with iconoclast poet Jim Simmerman, late Regents Professor at Northern Arizona University. She worked on-air at classical KNAU radio as a grad student earning her lowest-ever wage in one of the best-ever jobs. Her chapbooks *With Ridiculous Caution* (2013) and *O, But in the Library* (2017) were both published by Finishing Line Press. Having double-majored in English and music (vocal and instrumental), she is doubly fond of Renaissance and chance music.

www.ingramcontent.com/pod-product-compliance
Lightning Source LLC
Chambersburg PA
CBHW021149090426
42740CB00008B/1022